# SOUTH KOREA

**ABDO**
Publishing Company

# SOUTH KOREA

*by Racquel Foran*

**Content Consultant**
Balbina Hwang
Visiting Professor, Georgetown University

# CREDITS

Published by ABDO Publishing Company, PO Box 398166, Minneapolis, MN 55439.
Copyright © 2013 by Abdo Consulting Group, Inc. International copyrights reserved in all countries. No part of this book may be reproduced in any form without written permission from the publisher. The Essential Library™ is a trademark and logo of ABDO Publishing Company.

Printed in the United States of America,
North Mankato, Minnesota
102012
012013

 THIS BOOK CONTAINS AT LEAST 10% RECYCLED MATERIALS.

Editor: Arnold Ringstad
Series Designer: Emily Love

About the Author: Racquel Foran is a freelance writer living in Coquitlam, British Columbia, Canada. She enjoys writing about politics, current events, and social issues and is a frequent contributor to magazines and newspapers in her region.

**Cataloging-in-Publication Data**
Foran, Racquel.
 South Korea / Racquel Foran.
    p. cm. -- (Countries of the world)
Includes bibliographical references and index.
ISBN 978-1-61783-636-7
1. Korea (South)--Juvenile literature.   I. Title.
951.95--dc22
                                        2012946079

**Cover: Gyeongbokgung Palace in Seoul**

# TABLE OF CONTENTS

# CHAPTER 1
# A VISIT TO SOUTH KOREA

When you first started planning your trip to South Korea, you were excited to experience the vibrant capital city of Seoul, where more than 10 million people are packed into an area of slightly more than 230 square miles (596 sq km).[1] But after your nearly 12-hour flight from Seattle, Washington, to Seoul's Inchon International Airport, all you can think about is relaxing in one of the country's many bathhouses. You hope there is a *jjimjilbang*, or bathhouse, close to your hotel.

Although you have heard how modern and advanced South Korea is, the Inchon International Airport still surprises you. It is bright, sleek, and huge. The Airport Railway Express links the airport to downtown Seoul, but you decide to take a taxi to better

Inchon International served 34 million passengers in 2011. The airport employs 35,000 people.

**Inchon International Airport is among the busiest airports in the world.**

enjoy the scenery during the journey into the city. Upon first driving away from the airport, you are surprised to see how familiar many things are. The expressway leading away from the airport is surrounded by all the things you would expect to find: hotels, restaurants, car rental companies, and parking lots.

## KOREAN BATHHOUSES

A popular pastime in Korea is spending time relaxing at one of the many jjimjilbangs. In simple terms a jjimjilbang is a public bathhouse, but in reality it is much more than that. Guests enter a common lobby area where they pay a small entrance fee. In addition to traditional spa services such saunas, massages, and exercise rooms, there are also reading and sleeping rooms and an abundance of entertainment options, including movies, music, and restaurants. Many jjimjilbangs are open 24 hours a day, and foreign travelers have found they are both an excellent place to meet locals and an inexpensive, comfortable place to sleep for a night.

It doesn't take long for the landscape to shift, however, and soon you are driving through low hills scattered with farms, greenhouses, and small homes. Farther along, you can see the scenery is going to change again. The densely packed high-rises of downtown Seoul can be seen in the distance, and the traffic is becoming much heavier. Your excitement increases with each passing mile even as your progress on the increasingly busier streets slows.

**Seoul is South Korea's largest and most important city.**

**Political Boundaries of South Korea**

# SEOUL

Although there are many large cities in South Korea, Seoul far outstrips any other in terms of population and importance. For 600 years, the city has played an important role in shaping the culture and growth of the region. Situated on the Han River, Seoul is surrounded by mountains. In the late nineteenth century, it became one of the first Asian cities to have railways, trolley cars, and telephones.

More recently, Seoul has been lauded for its quick economic growth and inspiring ability to emerge from the ruin of the Korean War (1950–1953) and the division of the peninsula into North and South Korea. It has become a booming metropolis and global powerhouse in the new millennium. Now the city of Seoul is synonymous with global corporate names such as Samsung, LG,

## SHOPPER'S PARADISE

The city of Seoul offers a huge selection of shopping opportunities. The Myeong-dong district in particular represents the modern Korea. Hundreds of stores sell both Western and local brands. This is also the place to purchase cosmetics and skin care products. There are approximately 1,000 cosmetics shops in the district.[2] One of the district's department stores is a complex of several buildings, including luxury and youth fashion stores. There is also a hotel and a premium movie theater, where all the seats recline and where patrons are served food and beverages at their seats. More than 1 million people pass through Myeong-dong district each day.[3]

and Hyundai. It hosted the Olympic Games in 1988 and the FIFA World Cup in 2002.

By the time your taxi reaches the outer edges of the city, you are happy to see the sun is setting. The landscape is awash with flashing lights. High-rises sparkle in the night sky, and it seems as though every building is covered in bright neon signs. Because the buildings are packed so tightly together, the impact of the lights is magnified. It is difficult to make out the buildings behind these lights, so you are looking forward to seeing them in the daylight as well.

South Korea is a country of contrasts. Although the nation is small, it is difficult to traverse because of the extensive mountain ranges that cut through it in all directions. These mountains have relatively few inhabitants, though hundreds of Buddhist temples are scattered throughout them. The valleys are narrow, but the coastlines that surround three sides of the Korean Peninsula are long and the beaches are wide.

**In 2011, the average age of South Korea's ten tallest buildings was six years.**

South Korea is a country with an ancient history, experiencing rapid growth and modernization only in recent decades. This is reflected in the architecture, as modern high-rises stand shoulder to shoulder with historic buildings and fast-food restaurants. Millions of people live in urban centers surrounded by vast open

**The success of the Myeong-dong shopping district has led to the opening of similar shopping districts elsewhere in South Korea.**

**South Korea both cherishes its past and embraces the future.**

rice fields. The demilitarized zone (DMZ) between North and South Korea, created in the wake of the Korean War and perhaps the most heavily guarded border in the world today, is at the same time a sanctuary to many endangered plants and animals. The South Korean people have traditional values and strong cultural pride, but they also embrace modern technology and popular culture.

## SNAPSHOT

**Official name:** Republic of Korea (ROK) or South Korea

**Capital city:** Seoul

**Form of government:** republic

**Title of leaders:** president (head of state), prime minister (head of government)

**Currency:** South Korean won

**Population (July 2012 est.):** 48,860,500
*World rank:* 25

**Size:** 38,502 square miles (99,720 sq km)
*World rank:* 109

**Language:** Korean

**Official religion:** Almost 50 percent of the population claims no religion; 26.3 percent are Christian and 23.2 percent are Buddhist (1995 census)

**Per capita GDP (2011, US dollars):** $32,100
*World rank:* 40

## CHAPTER 2

# GEOGRAPHY: A VIRTUAL ISLAND

South Korea occupies 45 percent of East Asia's Korean Peninsula. It is surrounded on three sides by water. The Sea of Japan, also called the East Sea, is to the east, the Korea Strait to the south, and the Yellow Sea to the west. The 155-mile (250 km) DMZ running east to west across the center of the peninsula forms the border between South Korea and North Korea. Until the two countries reunite, South Korea is likely to remain a virtual island, unable to move its people or goods overland through North Korea to China and Russia.

**Koreans call the west and south coastlines *dadohae*, or "sea of many islands."**

**The South Korean coast on the Sea of Japan is less indented than the western coastline.**

# NEIGHBORS AND COASTS

South Korea covers an area of 38,023 square miles (99,720 sq km), making it slightly larger than the US state of Indiana.[1] Its nearest neighbor, other than North Korea, is Japan, which at its closest point lies approximately 70 miles (113 km) southwest of the Korean Peninsula. The Korean Peninsula's location between China and Japan and its proximity to the Pacific Ocean have had a major influence on Korean history and culture, as well as on South Korea's recent phenomenal economic growth.

The approximately 1,500 miles (2,413 km) of coastline that surrounds South Korea are diverse and dynamic.[2] Along the east coast, the mountains drop off quickly and steeply into the Sea of Japan, which averages more than 5,700 feet (1,700 m) deep.[3] There are no beaches where the mountains meet the sea directly, but in the places where streams run off mountainsides to the coast, scenic lagoons and sandy beaches can be found. The south and west coastlines are characterized by a series of bays, inlets, and natural indentations that make the true length of the coastline eight times longer than its straight-line

## NAMING DISPUTE

Though international agencies refer to the sea east of the Korean Peninsula as the Sea of Japan, both North Korea and South Korea refuse to accept this name. The governments of the two nations have lodged formal complaints in an attempt to get the name changed on official maps. Koreans instead refer to the body of water as the East Sea.

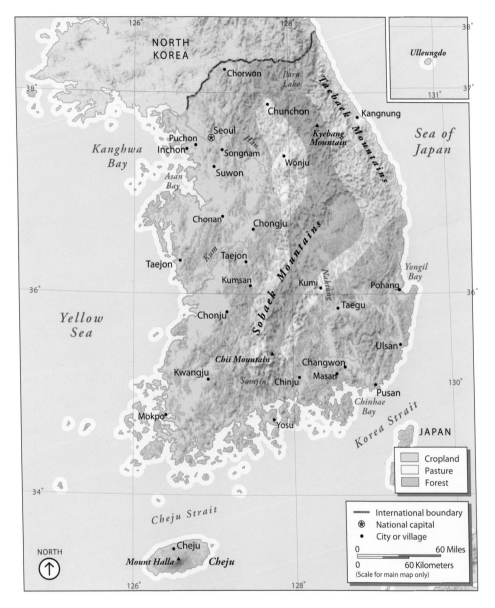

**Geography of South Korea**

distance.[4] These waters also feature more than 3,300 islands and islets, some of which are popular vacation spots for locals.[5] By far the largest island is Cheju, at 714 square miles (1,849 sq km).[6]

## MOUNTAINS, RIVERS, AND VALLEYS

Mountains are the dominant feature of the landscape in South Korea and the entire peninsula. The most prominent of the mountain ranges is the Taebaek, which begins in northeast North Korea and runs along the east coast into South Korea. This vast range divides the country into eastern and western sections, and it is the source of most of South Korea's important rivers. This includes the Han River, on which Seoul was built.

### THE HAWAII OF KOREA

Situated off the southwestern tip of the Korean Peninsula, Cheju Island is sometimes referred to as "the Hawaii of Korea." The core of the island is South Korea's highest peak, Mount Halla. The island is characterized by volcanic activity, with abundant crater-formed hills, waterfalls, and lava tunnels. The lava tunnels, along with Mount Halla itself, were named World Heritage Sites by the United Nations Educational, Scientific and Cultural Organization (UNESCO) in 2007. The waters surrounding Cheju Island are warm and turquoise blue, and the beaches are covered in golden sand, making it a popular vacation destination.

**A cable car carries passengers through the Taebaek Mountains.**

The mountains give the peninsula a tilted appearance; the highest mountains cluster in the northeast corner, where they drop suddenly into the Sea of Japan. On the southwestern side, the ranges slope more gradually to the Yellow Sea. Several large mountain chains branch off northeast and southwest from the Taebaek range. The largest of these in the southern part of South Korea is the Sobaek range. The high peaks here are the watersheds for most of the southern part of South Korea. The highest mountain in South Korea is a dormant volcano located in the center of Cheju Island called Mount Halla.

**Mount Halla stands 6,398 feet (1,950 m) tall.**

South Korea's major rivers—the Han, the Kum, the Naktong, and the Somjin—all have extensive plains extending out to sea. The plains are home to most South Korean agriculture. The flow of the rivers fluctuates depending on the season, with a tendency to flood the plains during the rainy monsoon season and run very low during most of the rest of the year. Major cities such as Seoul and Pusan lie on rivers. All of the major rivers flow west or south, with only small tributaries and streams flowing off the eastern ranges into the Sea of Japan.

## CLIMATE AND SEASONS

South Korea's seasons occur at the same time of year as in North America. The winter months of December through March can be bitterly cold in northern regions, but are relatively mild on the southern tip

## AVERAGE TEMPERATURE AND PRECIPITATION

| Region (City) | Average January Temperature Minimum/Maximum | Average July Temperature Minimum/Maximum | Average Precipitation January/July |
|---|---|---|---|
| Southwestern Plain (Seoul) | 21/33°F (-6/0°C) | 71/82°F (21/27°C) | 0.8/15.6 inches (2.1/39.5 cm) |
| Southwestern Plain (Mokpo) | 30/41°F (-1/5°C) | 72/81°F (22/27°C) | 1.5/7.8 inches (3.0/19.0 cm) |
| Southern Plain (Pohang) | 27/42°F (-2/5°C) | 70/82°F (21/27°C) | 1.4/7.3 inches (3.6/18.6 cm) |
| Central Mountains (Chinju) | 23/42°F (-5/6°C) | 69/82°F (21/28°C) | 1.3/12.1 inches (3.3/30.7 cm)[7] |

of the peninsula. The early part of summer is the rainy season, when monsoons from the Pacific Ocean are common. More rain falls from mid-June to mid-July than at any other time. The month of August tends to be extremely hot and humid. The coastlines offer many beautiful beaches that become popular escapes when heat and humidity become particularly harsh. In the fall, the trees outside the city come alive with

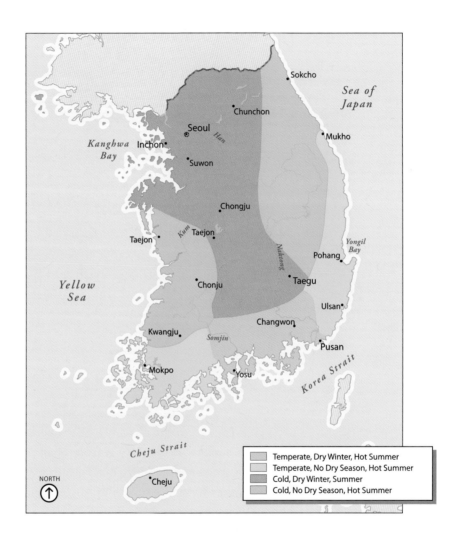

**Climate of South Korea**

hues of orange, yellow, and red. The weather is mild at this time of year; blue skies and comfortable temperatures are typical. Early spring, when cherry blossoms bloom, is also a pleasant time to visit.

## REGIONS AND URBAN SPACES

The country has nine provinces and seven large cities with provincial status and is informally divided into three broad regions. The central mountains region contains the Taebaek and Sobaek ranges. Small farming villages with terraced rice paddy farms are nestled in the valleys here. The region south of the central mountains is the southern plain. The landscape is gentler here, with rolling hills and extensive flood plains. Many farms are located in this region. Also in this region are many bays and fishing villages. The southwestern plain makes up the third region, which stretches from the southern tip of the peninsula to the Han River and Kanghwa Bay west of Seoul. Once a major farming region, much of its agricultural land has been lost to economic development and the expansion of urban centers.

South Korea loses 60 percent of its annual precipitation to runoff from floods during the rainy season.

Approximately 83 percent of South Korea's population now lives in urban centers.[9] Many cities have populations far exceeding 1 million people; almost 10 million people live in the capital city of Seoul alone.[10] South Korea has 16 ports, and most of its major cities have grown up around one of them.[11] This includes the country's second-largest city, Pusan, which possesses South Korea's largest port. The port of Inchon is the second largest in the country and is the gateway to Seoul.[12]

**Most South Koreans live in urban areas, including Seoul.**

# CHAPTER 3
# ANIMALS AND NATURE: ENDANGERED BY DEVELOPMENT

South Korea's landscape includes long coastlines, thousands of islands and islets, and vast mountain ranges, creating habitats for a wide variety of plants and animals. It is estimated there are more than 100,000 species living in the country, of which only 30,000 have been identified.[1] South Korea's rapid development has put many species at risk. In early 2012, the nation's Ministry of Environment added 25 species to its list of endangered species.[2]

In June 2012, two new species of sea horse were discovered in South Korean waters.

**The Siberian tiger is the unofficial national animal of South Korea.**

## ENDANGERED SPECIES IN SOUTH KOREA

According to the International Union for Conservation of Nature (IUCN), South Korea is home to the following numbers of species that are categorized by the organization as Critically Endangered, Endangered, or Vulnerable:

| | |
|---|---|
| Mammals | 9 |
| Birds | 29 |
| Reptiles | 1 |
| Amphibians | 1 |
| Fishes | 19 |
| Mollusks | 0 |
| Other Invertebrates | 3 |
| Plants | 5 |
| Total | 68[4] |

# ANIMALS

Once, the Korean Peninsula was a wild land. Deer, lynx, bears, and lions roamed freely in abundance. Species included the Siberian tiger, South Korea's unofficial national animal. There are more than 18,000 animal species in South Korea today, but only 123 are mammals.[3] Small rodents such as weasels are now common, but Siberian tigers, Korean wolves, and Eurasian lynx are all now either very rare or extinct. Asiatic black bears and leopards that were once abundant can now only be found in small numbers within the DMZ.

The coastal wetlands are also home to a large number of animals. More

South Korea's wetlands are an important habitat for migratory birds.

than 400 bird species can be found in the country, and the country's rice paddies, grassy marshes, and flood plains are a vital habitat to a number of migratory birds.[5] The migratory birds supported by this land include several threatened species, including the black-faced spoonbill.

**South Korea's mountainous regions are heavily forested.**

## FORESTS, TREES, AND PLANTS

In the early twentieth century, much of the Korean Peninsula was covered in forest. The landscape changed significantly between 1910 and 1945, when the region fell under Japanese colonial rule. During this time, the

Japanese stripped the land of its forests for timber and fuel. The Korean War caused even more devastation, and by the early 1960s vast regions lay bare. Recognizing a need to reverse the trend, the South Korean government established the Korea Forest Service in 1967. It undertook a massive reforestation project, resulting in more than 15,000 square miles (40,000 sq km) of land being rehabilitated; nearly 70 percent of the country is again covered with forests.[6]

## RIVER RESTORATION PROJECTS

One of the major projects on which the South Korean government has embarked as part of its green initiative is the redevelopment of four major rivers. The projects involve dredging and damming the rivers, with the objective of increasing the supply of freshwater to the region. At the same time, the effort aims to prevent regular floods. The plan also calls for the areas surrounding the rivers to be beautified with golf courses, bike trails, and park areas. However, some environmentalists are opposed to the plan. More than 50 species of migratory birds are dependent on the shallow river waters and flood plains, and environmentalists fear deepening the river waters will deplete feeding grounds and further endanger species such as the spoon-billed sandpiper.[7]

Forested areas are composed chiefly of coniferous trees, with the most common being pitch pine and Korean pine. Other species include spruces, larches, and yews. The rest of the forested areas contain a mix of deciduous trees and other types. Evergreen broad-leaved species such as camellias and camphor trees can be found along the southern coast and on Cheju Island. In the flatlands, orchards grow fruit trees, including pears and citrus fruits.

South Korea's plant life is not limited to the trees in its vast forests. Many beautiful and fragrant flowers flourish in the long humid summers, and South Koreans hold dozens of spring flower festivals throughout the country every year. Clematis, hibiscus, and orchids are among the spectacular blooms that brighten the country's landscape. The many coastal wetlands also offer an interesting variety of plants including dramatic Japanese blood grass.

## AIR QUALITY

In 2002, the Asian Institute for Energy, Environment, and Sustainability ranked South Korea 120 out of 122 countries for air quality.[8] Several government ministries worked closely with a number of nonprofit organizations and major automobile manufacturers to develop a plan to address air pollution. The government established emission reduction goals for factories, requiring them to cut their current levels in half by 2014. They are also encouraging vehicle owners to retire older, high-pollution cars early, and consider low-emission diesel vehicles as replacements. There are now 75 stations in the Seoul metropolitan area that monitor and record ozone, carbon monoxide, and other pollutants.[9] Electronic billboards in cities display air quality data for the public.

## PARKS AND GREEN SPACES

Perhaps because the country is so densely populated, South Koreans have an appreciation for nature and green spaces. The government recognizes

**Korea's large variety of flowers includes orchids.**

that a lack of green space in densely populated areas leads to poor air quality, among other environmental problems. In addition to the country's extensive reforestation efforts, the government has also established dozens of parks covering 7.8 percent of South Korea's territory, including 20 national parks, 30 provincial parks, and 33 county parks.[10] These parks cover diverse terrain and offer a wide range of topography. For example, Hallyeohaesang National Park and Dadohae National Park are both marine parks that encompass islands, the sea, and the mainland. Mount Bukhansan is the national park nearest to Seoul; just a subway ride away from the capital, it is a popular location for rock climbers.

## THE DMZ PRESERVES NATURE

Stretching 155 miles (250 km) across the Korean Peninsula, the DMZ between the two Koreas has become one of the world's greatest nature preserves. This no-man's-land traverses wetlands, forests, estuaries, and high mountain ranges. When the Korean War ended, all humans abandoned the land, leaving nature to reclaim it. Some have described it as one of the most dangerous safe places in the world—unsafe because of the land mines left over from the war, but a haven for plants and animals. Two-thirds of all of the peninsula's plant and animal life can be found in the DMZ.[11] It is home to almost 3,000 plants, more than 300 birds, and approximately 70 different mammals.[12] This pristine patch of land is also home to several endangered species, including the Asiatic black bear and a subspecies of the Siberian tiger, as well as two of the world's rarest birds, the white-naped and red-crowned cranes.

In addition to the parks, there are also several designated ecological and scenery conservation areas. More than 115 square miles (300 sq km) of land has been preserved in its

**The DMZ has become an unintentional nature preserve.**

natural state in an effort to protect sensitive habitats and places of scenic beauty.[13] Included in some of these preserved areas are primitive natural marshes, otter habitats, and coral structures.

## CHAPTER 4

# HISTORY: A NATION DIVIDED

Artifacts found in Manchuria, a region in northeast China, and in the Korean Peninsula indicate waves of people filtered down from Manchuria and Siberia onto the peninsula, where they settled along the coastline and river valleys of Korea approximately 500,000 years ago. However, scholars generally agree that today's Korean people are not descendants of these earliest people. The earliest artifacts of recognizably Korean culture date to approximately 8000 BCE. The people who made these artifacts became the ethnic foundation of the Korean people. Tombs found on the peninsula from the Bronze Age mark the tribal boundaries of the period and indicate there were many tribal states controlling the region.

The most powerful of these states was the Choson Kingdom, which was thriving by the fourth century BCE. Archaeologists have uncovered

**A young girl looks at a replica of an ancient Korean mural.**

## THE LEGEND OF TANGUN

According to legend, Korean history begins with Tangun. In the legend, the god Hwanung was sent to Earth to form a City of God by his father Hwanin, the ruler of Heaven. Once he arrived, he granted the wishes of a cave-dwelling bear and tiger that wished to become human. He gave each of them 20 cloves of garlic and a plant called mugwort, ordered them to eat only this, and told them to stay out of the sun for 100 days. The tiger gave up and left the cave early, but the bear succeeded and became a woman. Though she was grateful, she was lonely. Again Hwanung intervened, making her his wife. They had a son, Tangun, who established the Choson Kingdom. Mythological history claims he ruled for 1,500 years.

evidence that the Choson people developed advanced agricultural and military technology, including iron tools and weapons. The Chinese eventually overthrew the kingdom in 108 BCE.

## THE SILLA DYNASTY

In the first century BCE, three distinct kingdoms formed on the Korean Peninsula: Koguryo, Paekche, and Silla. Many of Korea's cultural and political traditions developed during this period. It was during this phase that Buddhism first became prevalent on the peninsula and was adopted as a state religion. In 668 CE, with the help of the Chinese, Silla overthrew the Paekche and Koguryo, unifying Korea. Soon after, Silla drove out the Chinese to form an absolute dynasty on the peninsula. Buddhism became the ideology around which the monarchy developed its power. The Chinese philosophy of Confucianism was also widely followed among aristocrats.

Silla ruled for hundreds of years before being overthrown. Paekche and Koguryo experienced brief resurgences. Eventually, General Wang Kon defeated Koguryo and founded the Koryo dynasty in 918. One of the greatest achievements of the Koryo dynasty was the invention of the first movable metal type in 1234. This allowed the quick printing of books and other written works. The achievement came more than 200 years before Johannes Gutenberg independently invented a similar device in Europe. It was also in the thirteenth century that Korean artisans carved the Buddhist scriptures into more than 80,000 wooden blocks in an effort to ward off Mongolian invaders with the help of Buddha.[1] Known as the Tripitaka Koreana, they are now national treasures and are preserved at the Haeinsa Temple.

The earliest surviving Korean book created with moveable metal type dates to 1377.

## THE CHOSON DYNASTY

In 1392, the power structure on the peninsula changed again when General Yi Song Gye overthrew Koryo and formed the Choson dynasty, named in honor of the most successful ancient Korean civilization. Yi Song Gye established his capital at Hanyang, now the capital city Seoul. The Choson dynasty pulled away from Buddhist influences in government and leaned more toward the teachings of Confucius. It was the most successful and longest running of all the Korean dynasties. During its period of rule from 1392 to 1910, the Choson dynasty created the Korean alphabet, known as Hangul, and established a bureaucratic

administrative system. And, as is common in the history of the Korean Peninsula, it also had to fight off several attempted invasions.

When Japan invaded in 1592, Korean land forces suffered defeats and major damage was done to cities. Palaces and public buildings were burned to the ground, and cultural treasures were destroyed. Korea did, however, have success on the water. They had invented advanced new warships, known as turtle ships. Turtle ships had spiked metal tops to prevent boarding by enemy sailors. They also had carved dragon heads mounted at the ship's front, which frightened the enemy and could release a thick, toxic smoke to block the enemy's vision. With the help of these new weapons, they won key naval battles and eventually defeated the Japanese.

The Manchu people of northeast China encroached on Korea's northern border in the early seventeenth century, resulting in a quarter century of conflict among the Manchu, the Koreans, and the Chinese. These frequent invasions caused Korea to turn inward, maintaining ties only with Japan and China. Korea began to gain a reputation of being a so-called hermit kingdom.

**The largest turtle ship was 110 feet (33.5 m) long and 28 feet (8.5 m) wide.**

**Kyongbok Palace was originally built in 1394 and was reconstructed in the nineteenth century.**

## JAPANESE COLONIZATION AND RULE

Throughout the nineteenth century, many nations competed for power in East Asia. Though the Choson dynasty was still independent, the Qing dynasty of China had exerted influence and demanded tribute from Korea since the seventeenth century. However, after successive attacks from France, Britain, and Russia, the Chinese were quickly losing their power. At the same time, the Japanese were working hard to modernize, while Korea had closed itself off from the world and stalled its development. The Japanese took advantage of these factors and in 1876 threatened Korea, forcing it to sign an unequal treaty giving Japanese merchants and sailors favorable treatment on Korean waters and lands. The treaty also opened previously closed Korean ports to Japanese trade. China did not stand by idly. In an effort to dilute Japanese control, they encouraged Korea to further open its trade relations. Within ten years, Korea had signed treaties with Britain, the United States, and Russia.

This opening up of Korea prompted a campaign within the country to wrest Korea from foreign influence and control. The Independence Club was formed, and the first newspaper written in the Hangul language, called Tongnip simmun, or *The Independent*, was produced to advocate an end to foreign control. Among the student leaders in the reform movement was Syngman Rhee, who later became South Korea's first president. Korea asked China for assistance in expelling the Japanese, but the request gave Japan an excuse to move troops onto the peninsula, igniting the first Sino-Japanese War (1894–1895). The Japanese prevailed

**Syngman Rhee, a student protester, was later South Korea's first president.**

against the Chinese, taking another step toward winning complete control of the peninsula.

At the same time the Japanese took control of the peninsula, Russia was also increasing its influence in East Asia. Russia allied with France and

Germany to force Japan into returning control of the Liaodong Peninsula to China. As soon as China again gained control of the peninsula, they leased it to Russia. The Russians also signed a Sino-Russian treaty in 1896, permitting Russia to build and operate the Chinese Eastern Railway through northern Manchuria. This railway served as a vital link to the Russian Trans-Siberian Railway into Vladivostok, a city near Russia's borders with China and Korea. These moves by Russia eventually led to the Russo-Japanese War (1904–1905). Once again, the rapidly modernized Japanese were victorious. As part of the peace treaty, Russia acknowledged Japan's "paramount political, military, and economic interest" in Korea.[2] A few years later, in 1910, Japan annexed Korea as a colony.

Once Korea was under Japan's total control, the Japanese moved quickly to eradicate Korean culture, history, and national pride. Everything Korea did was now secondary to Japan's needs, and all Korean methods of doing things were replaced with Japanese systems. Japanese modern education replaced Confucianism, colonial rule replaced independent Korean administration, and Japanese replaced Korean as the language. Japanese bureaucracies controlled industrial and agricultural projects, eventually making use of much of Korea's fertile land. Japanese occupiers created laws legitimizing discrimination against Koreans. After centuries of growth and independence, Koreans had become second-class citizens on the peninsula.

**Under Japanese rule, Koreans were not allowed to publish their own newspapers.**

**The Russo-Japanese War led to Japanese rule over Korea.**

## WORLD WAR II

In 1937, Japan went to war with China. Following the December 1941 attack on Pearl Harbor, it also went to war with the United States, bringing the United States into World War II (1939–1945). The war was fought between the Axis powers, including Japan, Germany, and Italy, and the Allied powers, including the United States, the United Kingdom, and the Soviet Union. The Soviet Union included the country formerly known as Russia. The war effort shifted the roles of many Koreans. The labor shortage left behind by soldiers created bureaucratic and administrative opportunities for Koreans that had not existed before. But this also had the effect of creating class divisions. Many Koreans who suffered badly at the hands of the Japanese believed those who enhanced their standing in Korean society during this time were Japanese collaborators. The issue divided people, even within families.

The Korean Peninsula continued to be of great interest to other powers. Many believed the Soviet Union in particular was interested in controlling the peninsula, since capturing it would give it access to a warm-water port and the Pacific Ocean. The Soviets allowed guerilla forces to hide and train along the Chinese-Russian border.

Prior to the Japanese surrender in September 1945, the Allies had decided that when Japan did surrender, Korea would become independent "in due course."[3] Because the United States did not trust the Soviets with complete control of the peninsula, and the Soviet Union did not want the United States to have complete control, the United States proposed splitting the country into northern and southern regions at the 38th parallel. The Soviets took control of the north and the Americans of the south in late 1945. It was supposed to be a temporary measure, but mistrust between the two nations ultimately led to a cold war in Korea. Soviet troops marched into North Korea alongside Korean fighters in August 1945 and occupied the territory.

With Korea divided, the American occupiers of the south wanted to find a leader they were comfortable with. Syngman Rhee was familiar to the United States. The former student activist had been the leader of Korea's government-in-exile during Japanese rule, and he had been living in the United States for many years, actively campaigning for a unified Korea. On May 10, 1948, the South Korean National Assembly elected Rhee as president, and on August

## SYNGMAN RHEE

Though he later became a dictatorial leader and was forced to resign under accusations of election fraud, Syngman Rhee's early years were impressive. In 1896, Rhee joined with other young Koreans to form the Independence Club. The club's purpose was to resist Japanese rule in Korea. His activism led to him spending six years in prison. When he was finally released, he moved to the United States, where he was the first Korean to earn a PhD from the prestigious Princeton University in New Jersey. He later moved to Hawaii and from there championed Korean independence. In 1919, while still in Hawaii, he was elected president of the Korean Provisional Government. He spent several years in this position before he was pushed out. He then moved to Washington DC during World War II, where he became familiar to the Americans who eventually put him in power in South Korea.

15 the newly established Republic of Korea (ROK) officially formed its first government.

## THE KOREAN WAR

Koreans were angered by the split-country arrangement that was forced upon them. Unifying the peninsula became a common political drive for both North and South once Korea was divided. Unfortunately, each side was determined to achieve unification through force and under its own system. By early 1949, Kim Il Sung had consolidated his power in North Korea, making himself the prime minister of the new nation. He fortified the 38th parallel and regularly carried out maneuvering drills along the border. South Korean president Syngman Rhee, elected in 1948, also talked of uniting the peninsula by force. Neither the North nor the South recognized the 38th parallel as a real border, and small battles, instigated by both sides, started to break out along the line on a regular basis.

These small clashes turned to war on June 25, 1950, when Kim Il Sung crossed the 38th parallel with his Korean People's Army (KPA) and drove South Korean forces to the southern tip of the peninsula. Taken by surprise, the southern forces quickly collapsed. If not for the last-minute intervention of the United Nations (UN), led by the United States, the entire peninsula likely would have fallen to North Korean rule. With the help of UN forces, composed mostly of US troops, the

**The Korean War resulted in tremendous damage to cities and thousands of deaths.**

KPA was driven north, well past the 38th parallel, all the way to the North Korea–China border. Chinese troops rallied and pushed the UN forces out of the North. Two long years of battles without progress or movement ensued. Finally, on July 27, 1953, the UN Command and the KPA signed an armistice, and a demilitarized zone along the 38th parallel was established. Since the agreement was only an armistice and not a peace treaty, the two Koreas are still technically at war. Continual instability in the peninsula has resulted in the continued presence of US troops in South Korea.

In July 1953, thousands of prisoners of war were returned in Operation Big Switch.

The Korean War left the entire peninsula in ruins. Buildings and historic treasures were destroyed, forests were stripped bare, and millions were killed or wounded. The two Koreas were even more polarized, and the possibility of a quick, peaceful reunification was lost. Leaders on both sides of the 38th parallel were faced with the enormous task of rebuilding their nations, but they took very different approaches.

## THE REPUBLICS

After Syngman Rhee's election, he took on dictatorial powers; from the beginning of his first term, the opposition party worked hard to unseat him. When the opposition introduced a vote to shift to a parliamentary style of government in 1952, Rhee declared martial law. He called in the members of the National Assembly and forced a vote on the issue of electing a president by popular vote. All but three of the 166 members

**Demonstrations against the South Korean leadership broke out in the 1960s.**

voted in favor of the change, and later that year Rhee won the election with 72 percent of the vote.[4]

The constitution did still limit the number of terms a president could serve. Rhee used his power to change the constitution in his favor, allowing him to continue as president. The Korean people who had fought so long and so hard for independence began objecting to Rhee's fraudulent methods and dictatorial style. Civilians began staging uprisings against the government. The best known of these took

## TEN DAYS IN MAY

After the Korean War ended, it took several decades for the country to establish democratic political stability. South Koreans were vocal about their desire for democracy during this time. One of the most tragic incidents to occur during these transitional years took place in 1980. Pro-democracy demonstrations were increasing in size and number throughout the country, and the city of Kwangju was particularly active. In response to this, on May 17, 1980, the government declared martial law and sent paratroopers into the cities to break up demonstrations. In Kwangju, shots were fired into the air, killing many, and people were beaten on the streets. Even innocent bystanders suffered at the hands of the paratroopers. In the end, hundreds died during what is now known as the Kwangju Massacre.[6]

place on April 19, 1960, when the police killed 142 people during a student protest.[5] The South Korean and US governments urged Rhee to step down, and he resigned later that month, bringing an end to the First Republic.

The Second Republic was short-lived. Only a year after establishing a new parliamentary system, a military coup overthrew the ruling Democratic Party in 1961. This signaled the beginning of 32 years of military control of the ROK. The leader of the coup, Major General Park Chung Hee, amended the constitution to allow his reelection four times before he was assassinated in 1979. Park is given credit for his role in South Korea's economic development, but he ruled with harsh authority, restricting personal freedom, interfering with the courts, and trying to silence the press.

From 1979 to 1980, Choi Kyu Hah was president in name. However, when military forces declared martial law in response to civil unrest, General Chun Doo Hwan took control of the country. He was elected in 1980 and in 1981 repealed martial law. President Chun promised the people the constitution would be changed so the president would be limited to a single seven-year term. Although he hesitated to follow through on this promise at first, attempting to appoint his close associate Roh Tae Woo as his successor, he eventually caved to widespread protests and agreed to change the constitution. In 1988, Roh Tae Woo was the first president elected under the new constitution.

Under the new government, South Korea experienced international attention when Seoul hosted the 1988 Summer Olympic Games. The constitutional changes also brought improved civil liberties, but the economy stalled. There was little doubt by this time, however, that the next election would be a fully democratic one.

## VOTING FOR CHANGE

In February 1993, the South Korean people elected the first nonmilitary government in more than 30 years. Among the great accomplishments of President Kim Young Sam were the first local and provincial direct vote elections since 1961. In 1995, local citizens directly elected thousands of mayors, provincial governors, and local officials.

South Korea ran into a major difficulty during the 1997 Asian financial crisis. Several nations in East and Southeast Asia saw their currencies decrease in value, their stock markets drop, and their debts increase. International agencies stepped in to provide emergency loans to South Korea, and new regulations were put into place to ensure that a similar crisis would not happen again.

In 1998, the first opposition party leader was elected as president. Kim Dae Jung wanted to take South Korea in a new direction. In his inauguration speech, referring to difficult economic times, he said, "Let us open a new age during which we will overcome the national crisis and make a new leap forward."[7] Within two years, he had almost doubled economic growth and halved unemployment, speeding the recovery from the 1997 financial crisis. Under his so-called Sunshine Policy, Kim also sought to improve relations with North Korea. These efforts culminated in an unprecedented meeting with Kim Jong Il, Kim Il Sung's son and successor, in Pyongyang in 2000.

The 2002 elections brought President Roh Moo Hyun into power. He was a progressive who appealed to young voters due to his platform as a reformist. He supported the previous administration's conciliatory

## THE SUNSHINE POLICY

When President Kim Dae Jung won the 1998 election, he focused on reestablishing relations with North Korea. His sunshine policy included reuniting separated families, increasing cultural and academic exchanges, and improving economic ties with North Korea. In 2000, he was awarded a Nobel Peace Prize for his efforts, but he did not see his ultimate goal of harmonious relations realized by the time of his death in 2009.

**Kim Dae Jung originally entered politics during the administration of Syngman Rhee.**

approach to North Korea and vowed to end the systemic problem of corruption in government and business. He had little success in most areas, and voters rejected his party in the next election.

The 2007 elections saw a businessman elected as president for the first time. Lee Myung Bak, a former Hyundai executive, won the election in a landslide. However, only 63 percent of eligible voters cast a ballot.[8] This represented the lowest voter turnout since the country's first democratic elections.

# CHAPTER 5
# PEOPLE: AN AGING POPULATION

Many of the underlying values and traditions of South Korea stem from the concepts of hierarchy, humility, and harmony. The Confucian philosophy, which played a significant role in Korea's development, has always held respect for elders as one of its most important values. In Korea, the elderly are revered and their wisdom is rarely challenged. To treat an older person in a casual manner is regarded as disrespectful. Korean culture also emphasizes modesty. Talking about accomplishments is considered to show a lack of humility. Maintaining harmony is also important, and Koreans are often willing to compromise in order to keep harmonious relationships. These deeply entrenched values likely go a long way in keeping order in the very crowded country.

It is rude to wear shoes inside South Korean homes; guests should leave their shoes by the door.

**A group of children celebrates South Korea's Independence Day.**

### *GIBUN* **AND** *NUNCHI*

*Gibun*, roughly translated to "feelings," are what South Koreans use to gauge other people's mood or state of mind. South Koreans consider it very rude to offend someone's gibun. Maintaining harmony in relationships takes precedence over all else; it is considered crass to place honesty, efficiency, or anything else over harmony. *Nunchi*, or intuition, is a cultural sense that Koreans have developed to gauge another person's gibun. It is sometimes unclear to foreigners what Koreans find offensive, but understanding gibun can help them better understand Korean social interactions.

## DEMOGRAPHICS

Urban centers throughout South Korea are very busy with foot and vehicle traffic, but there is a noticeable lack of children. Many young adults delay starting families, and some choose not to have children at all. South Korea has one of the lowest birthrates in the world, with an estimated 8.42 births per 1,000 people in 2012. By comparison, the rate was 13.68 in the United States for that year.

In developing nations the number can reach more than 40.[1] As a result of South Korea's low birthrate, population growth has virtually stalled. It is estimated the population will grow by less than one-quarter of a percent in 2012.[2] Some politicians have started to vocalize their concern about the impact this will have on South Korea's economic growth, asking the government to encourage people to have more children by offering day care options and lowering education costs.

The median age of the South Korean population in 2012 was 39 years, meaning that a large proportion of people will be reaching

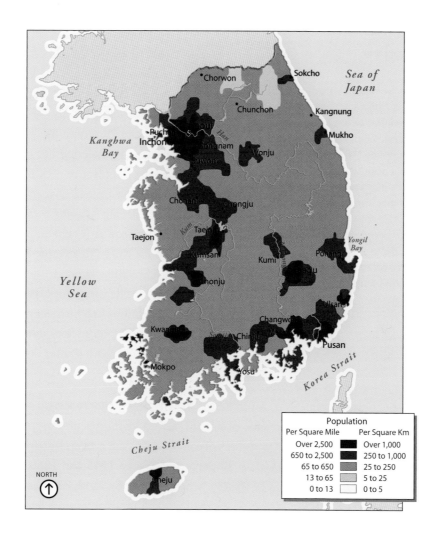

**Population Density of South Korea**

## POPULATION DENSITY

South Korea is one of the most densely populated countries in the world. It is ranked 109 in the world in terms of total area, but twenty-fifth in the world for population. Nearly 49 million people live on less than 38,615 square miles (100,000 sq km) of land, giving the country a population density of approximately 1,240 people per square mile (480 people per sq km). By comparison, the population density in the United States is approximately 80 people per square mile (32 people per sq km).[6] The city of Seoul is particularly crowded, with nearly 10 million people crowded into just under 250 square miles (650 sq km), making it far more densely populated than New York City, Tokyo, or London.[7]

retirement age over the next 25 to 30 years.[3] Retirees are living longer too, with the average Korean expected to live until age 79.[4] With its relatively small number of young people, the nation is expected to face challenges in replacing its aging workforce as it retires. South Korea has avoided using immigration to replace its aging population; it continues to be a very homogenous society, and few foreigners live in the country.

Since the Korean War, South Korea has become an increasingly urban population. The first wave of people moved from agricultural regions after World War II and the Korean War to take jobs in factories. The population of the cities grew 30 percent between 1945 and 1960, and this population shift has been steady ever since.[5] By 2012, 83 percent of the nation's total population of approximately 50 million people lived in one of the country's huge urban centers.[8] There are now several cities

**South Korean cities are very densely packed.**

with a population in excess of 1 million people and more than one-fifth of
the nation's population lives in Seoul alone.[9]

# LANGUAGE

All South Koreans speak the Korean language. There are approximately 70 million speakers of Korean in the world, and almost all of them live on the Korean Peninsula.[10] Some foreign influences can be seen and heard in the language. A few Chinese ideograms are still present, and since US troops arrived in the 1950s, more and more English words and American expressions can be heard in the spoken language. Learning English is considered important, and most children are taught the language in school. Courses in the languages of China are also available at schools in Seoul.

## THE KOREAN ALPHABET

During the Choson dynasty, King Sejong created the Hangul alphabet to provide a writing system for commoners who could not read or write Chinese. The alphabet consists of 24 symbols representing letters, including both consonants and vowels. Different letters can be combined into a single, more complex character representing a syllable. In a manual published in 1446 to explain the new script, King Sejong offered the following reasoning for creating it: "Being of foreign origin, Chinese characters are incapable of capturing uniquely Korean meanings. Therefore, many common people have no way to express their thoughts and feelings. Out of my sympathy for their difficulties, I have created a set of twenty-eight letters. The letters are very easy to learn, and it is my fervent hope that they improve the quality of life of all people."[11]

## RELIGIONS

Religious freedom is guaranteed by the South Korean constitution, and the nation does not have an official religious

## YOU SAY IT!

| English | Korean |
|---|---|
| Hello | Anyonghaseyo (uhn-YOHNG-hah-see-yoh) |
| Good-bye | Annyonghi gaseyo (uhn-NYOHNG-heye gah-see-yoh) |
| Thank you | Kamsahamnida (KAM-sah-ham-neye-dah) |
| You're welcome | Anieyo (UH-neye-ee-yoh) |
| How are you? | Chal jinaeshossoyo (CHAL jeye-nay-shoh-soh-yoh) |
| Good morning | Annyonghaseyo (uhn-NYOHNG-huh-see-yoh) |
| Good night | Anyonghi jumuseyo (uhn-YOHNG-heye joo-moo-see-yoh) |

South Koreans do not advance their age on their birthday, but rather each year on New Year's Day.

affiliation. However, religion has long played a role in Korean life and there are several diverse religions actively practiced in South Korea. The three most common religions are Christianity, Buddhism, and Shamanism. More than 26 percent of the population claim Christian affiliation, and another 24 percent say they are Buddhist.[12] Almost half the population claims no religious affiliation at all, but it is not unusual to find both worshippers and non-worshippers seeking the counsel of a shaman.

Shamanism, the worship of spirits that live in natural places such as rivers, lakes, trees, and mountains, is Korea's oldest religion, although some argue it is not a religion at all. Because there is no moral or spiritual ideal associated with it and no promise of salvation, Western scholars tend to view shamanism more as medicine than religion. Either way, shamans still exist; Koreans hire shamans to call on spirits to bring prosperity to their household or ward off evil spirits to cure an illness. For many years the Korean government tried to discourage the people from believing in shamans, and they tried to hide from foreigners many of the rituals tied to shamanism. With growth, urbanization, and modernization, however, the government has recognized that these rituals and practices hold cultural and historical importance. Recently, introducing these traditions to the younger generation has been encouraged.

**Shamans remain a part of modern Korean culture.**

# FAMILY STRUCTURES

Confucianism has also had a major influence on the Korean people. Devotion to the father from the son, as expressed in Confucian teachings, has long been the foundation of Korean families. Having a male family heir was, and often still is, of the utmost importance. It is the son who is responsible for carrying on family traditions, and when the father dies, the oldest son inherits the family home and most of the family money. This tradition undervalued daughters and severely undermined the role of women in society.

Things have slowly started to change. Many families were split apart after the Korean War because of both the division of the country and increased urbanization. The population shift from the country to the city has changed family structures and dynamics. Large

## WOMEN'S RIGHTS

One of the more negative legacies of a Confucian-based society is the inequality of women. For many centuries in South Korea, boys were provided a better education and were given more opportunities to enter into government positions than girls. Men ran households, and women needed their husband, father, or son to sign legal documents on their behalf. Once married, mothers-in-law controlled their new daughters.

Modern Korean women are experiencing more and more equality. They now have equal access to education, and when married, they are no longer under the control of their in-laws. Still, sons are often preferred over daughters, there are still more men than women in politics and executive positions, and women tend to be laid off from jobs before men.

**A couple gets married in the traditional style.**

multigenerational family units no longer live together as they used to, and children are more likely to move away from their parents to seek opportunities in different cities, provinces, or even countries. Along with these changes, equality among the sexes is gradually improving. The first female presidential candidate, Park Geun Hye, ran for the office in December 2012.

## CHAPTER 6

# CULTURE: HOLDING ON TO TRADITIONS

South Koreans like to celebrate. Many festivals are held each year in South Korea to honor historic people or events. These festivals usually involve traditional costumes and reenactments of important moments in history. One of the best examples is the Baekje Cultural Festival. It was founded in October 1995 to celebrate the ancient Paekche kings; hundreds of celebrations are held every year, alternating locations between Buyeo and Gongju. There are memorial ceremonies in honor of the kings who reigned during the Paekche dynasty, as well as reenactments of throne succession ceremonies and historical street parades.

**In May, temples light colorful lanterns during the Lotus Lantern Festival.**

South Koreans also celebrate a wide variety of cultural and natural events at festivals held throughout the country. For those who want to start the year off with peaceful scenery, the Jeongdongjin

**A parade of women celebrates a holiday in honor of Buddha.**

and Homigot Sunrise Festivals held on December 31 and January 1 are very popular events. Later in January, South Koreans celebrate winter at the Hwacheon Sancheoneo, or Mountain Trout, Ice Festival. Cultural experiences such as ice fishing and sledding are among the popular activities people enjoy. The spring months bring flower and insect festivals, including the Hampyeong Butterfly Festival, the Muju Firefly Festival, the Hangang Yeouido Spring Flower Festival, and the Jinhae Gunhangje Cherry Blossom Festival. Festivals are held to celebrate teas, mimes, films, travel, fabrics, music, whales, and octopuses—to name just a few examples.

One of Korea's most celebrated holidays, Dano, is recognized by the Gungneung Danoje Festival. It features shamanic rituals dedicated to agriculture. In them, the shaman prays for abundant harvests, along with peace and health for the people. The festival has been recognized by both the UN and South Korea itself as an important component of the nation's heritage.

There are also ten public national holidays celebrated annually in South Korea, including New Year's Day, Children's Day on May 5, and Christmas Day. In the port city of Pusan, Christmas is celebrated with a tree-lighting festival every year. Another holiday, Chuseok, is a harvest celebration. It does not have a set calendar date; instead, the date on which it is held is determined by the lunar calendar. Typically, it occurs in early autumn.

**A diver in a Santa Claus suit holds up a sign reading "Merry Christmas" in an aquarium in Seoul.**

## TRADITIONAL PERFORMANCES

An important part of many holidays and cultural events are dances, which often feature a variety of masks. The Gwanno Mask Drama is a popular example. It is a lighthearted drama in which the lower-class servants wear masks of the upper-class nobles. They act out a nonverbal love story about the noble class that includes conflict and humor.

Another well-known cultural dance is the Hahoe Mask Dance Drama, which dates to the mid-twelfth century. The dance is part of a shamanic ritual to bring peace and prosperity to the people. In ten acts, the performers play out themes while wearing masks to represent people in society—for example, a blushing bride or greedy aristocrat. The themes of the drama almost always poke fun at the ruling class.

## MUSIC

Traditional folk music plays an important role in many performances and celebrations. There are three styles of folk songs whose origins are regionally based: Namdo minyo, mournful songs, are from the southwest. Gyeonggi minyo are happier songs that come from the central region. Seodo minyo songs, from the northwest, have a nasal tone. Vocal performances called *pansori* are also popular.

In fan dances, women use large fans to form shapes such as butterflies, blooming flowers, and rolling surfs.

**Traditional Korean fan dances feature brightly colored clothing.**

These performances involve a drummer and a single performer holding a fan and handkerchief. The singer tells stories using a combination of dramatic action and singing; some performances last up to five hours.

South Korean music has a distinctive sound because so many of the instruments used are unique to the culture. The *changgo* drum is almost always heard in Korean music. It has a large hourglass-shaped body made of wood, and it is covered on each end with ox or horse skin. The musician plays it by striking each end with sticks or a stick and a hand. The *daegeum* is a bamboo flute that can be heard in folk music. Similar to many Korean instruments, a legend exists surrounding its invention. In the legend, King Sinmun instructed artisans to make the flute from special bamboo to restore peace in the Silla kingdom. Other instruments often heard in Korean folk music include the *piri*, a large double-reed oboe, the *haegeum*, an instrument similar to a fiddle, and the *pyeonjong*, a bronze bell.

The stars of modern Korean pop music, or K-pop, create the same kind of fan hysteria as teen pop idols in the United States and United Kingdom. Concerts draw massive crowds, and girls scream in frenzy at the sight of their favorite celebrities. The music is generally upbeat, singing groups usually have many members, performances include elaborate dance numbers, and every performer is stylized to establish and promote the latest fashion trends. These music groups infiltrate every branch of media.

**South Korean rapper PSY had a worldwide hit in 2012 with his song "Gangnam Style."**

## ART AND ARCHITECTURE

With such a long history, it is no surprise that great diversity can be found in Korea's art and literature. Each era of the peninsula's history contributed something different to Korea's artistic palette. The Paekche dynasty showed particular skill at crafting gold accessories and detailed Buddhist statues. And one of the greatest pieces of Korean art came from Silla: the monumental statue of the Buddha located in the Seokguram Grotto. Established in the eighth century and recognized as a UNESCO World Heritage Site in 1995, the Seokguram Grotto also features portrayals of gods and disciples sculpted into the walls surrounding Buddha. The detail and realism of the sculptures have resulted in their status as masterpieces of Buddhist art in the Far East.

### THE SEOUL ARTS CENTER

The Seoul Arts Center and Opera House is South Korea's first multidisciplinary arts and cultural center. The enormous complex was built in three phases over five years. Completed in 1993, it is home to a massive opera theater, concert and recital halls, an art gallery, a film archive, and an art library.

Traditional Korean housing did not change for hundreds of years. People lived in simple *hanoks*, or traditional houses, roofed with thatches, shingles or tiles. The houses varied in shape, but in all cases the design was practical and environmentally sound. Hanok houses are heated using a system called *ondol*, in which heat from cooking

**The construction of hanoks varies depending on the regions in which they are built and on their orientation within the landscape.**

stoves is channeled under the home to heat stone under the floor. The heat then rises to warm the whole house. In the summer, doors and windows are left open to create natural cross breezes that cool the home. All hanok houses are made from natural materials. Pillars, rafters, doors, and floors are made from wood. Walls are made from a mixture of earth and grass, and paper is used as windows and room dividers. The floors are sealed with bean oil to make them waterproof. Hanok houses place importance on courtyards and outdoor spaces, and they were designed to blend in with their natural environment. Rapid development has resulted in many of these traditional homes being torn down.

In recent decades, South Korea has embarked on building projects that have garnered international recognition. The Leeum Samsung Museum of Art is a fine example of how architects are once again finding a balance between the traditional values of harmoniously fitting structures into their environment and modern design elements and practicalities. Paju Book City is a good example of the government using architecture to revitalize a region and an industry. In an effort to stimulate and centralize the publishing industry, the government built a new city on reclaimed wetlands. Construction began in 1989, with the government inviting architects from all over the world to design buildings for the new urban center. The complex is now home to a thriving publishing industry.

## FOOD

Unlike citizens of most Western countries, Koreans distinguish breakfast, lunch, and dinner not by the kind of food they eat, but rather by the portion size. Meals tend to get larger later in the day. In addition to rice, most meals include soup and kimchi. Kimchi—a spicy, pickled vegetable dish—is the best-known element of Korean cuisine. It can be made from almost any vegetable, but cabbage is most commonly used. Kimchi was

**Kimchi is eaten both by itself and as a part of many other dishes.**

first made as a way to preserve vegetables through the long winters. The cabbage is mixed with spices, ginger, peppers, garlic, and green onion, and put in pots deep in the ground to ferment over the winter. Kimchi recipes can vary a great deal from family to family and from region to region. Since the taste changes quite a bit during the fermenting process, most people have a preference for kimchi of a specific age.

South Korean meals tend to emphasize vegetables, and many dishes are presented in a way that brings out the colors and scents of the food. Fish and meat are used sparingly. Although Korean cooking uses some common ingredients with Chinese and Japanese cooking, it tends to be less salty than Japanese food and less oily than Chinese food. One popular South Korean dish is a rice bowl with vegetables, red pepper paste, and a softly cooked egg called *bee bim bap*. *Chop chae*, another favorite, is a mix of clear noodles and chopped meat and vegetables. Another dish is a sushi-like roll called *kim bap* that has strips of vegetables and seasoned rice wrapped in a Korean seaweed called *kim*. The diversity of ingredients used in recipes has helped to increase the popularity of Korean food in Western cultures, and Korean restaurants are now a common sight in many North American cities.

## INTERNATIONAL SPORTS EVENTS

Winning the bid to host the 1988 Summer Olympics in Seoul was a major achievement for the country. The event gave the rest of the world a close-up look at a rebuilt South Korea. The trend that began with the Olympics continued with the FIFA World Cup. Cohosted in 2002 with Japan, the event was a resounding success. The South Korean team exceeded expectations, making it all the way to the semifinals. Foreign media were amazed by the size of the local crowds of fans; it was estimated that almost 22 million people gathered on the streets of South Korea to cheer on their soccer team.[1] Internationally, it was agreed that though the South Korean team lost, the success of the event was a major victory for the nation.

## SPORTS

Influences from both the ancient and modern worlds can be found in Korean sports. Tae Kwon Do, a martial art that uses both the hands and feet,

**Tae Kwon Do is a popular sport around the world.**

is the best-known Korean sport. *Ssireum* is a traditional Korean folk competition that is still practiced. Two players wearing sashes tied around their waists and thighs wrestle each other to the ground by using the sash as leverage for maneuvers. South Koreans also enjoy many Western

## KITE FLYING

The first kites were created approximately 3,000 years ago, but no one knows for sure where they were invented. They first appeared in Korean history in approximately 637 CE. Kites were used for a wide variety of purposes, such as sending messages, raising banners, spying on enemies, and measuring weather. In modern times, they are generally used for leisure. Koreans consider kite flying a sport, and some enthusiasts even participate in kite flying tournaments. Tournament categories include kite fighting and sport kite ballet.

sports. Baseball, golf, swimming, and figure skating are particularly popular.

The development of South Korean sports in recent decades has gone hand-in-hand with the nation's overall pace of development. The Korean National Baseball team has been successful in recent years, winning a gold medal at the Beijing Olympics in 2008 and a silver medal at the World Baseball Classic in 2009. Women in particular have excelled in golf, with professional golfer Se Ri Pak winning several Ladies Professional Golf Association (LPGA) championships. Park Tae Hwan is one of the country's world-class swimmers. He has won four Olympic medals, including a gold medal at the Beijing Olympics—the first Korean swimmer to achieve this.[2] The 2012 Summer Olympics in London also saw South Korean triumphs, with gold medals in archery, judo, and shooting. The nation's athletes won 28 medals in all, including 13 gold medals.[3]

**Kite flying is a popular sport in South Korea.**

## CINEMA

Records indicate that many films were made in Korea between 1920 and 1945, but few survived the Korean War. Only a few films from the period between the division of the peninsula and the end of the Korean War still exist. It was not until after the end of the Korean War and with the help of the South Korean government that the film industry started growing. The most talented directors of the time were not afraid to address social taboos and challenge Confucian conservatism.

It was difficult for the industry to grow, however, because of continual political instability and interference. Though a number of high quality films were produced throughout the 1960s, 1970s, and 1980s, it was not until the 1990s that the film industry really began experiencing true freedom of expression. The movie industry in South Korea has been on the rise ever since, with South Koreans showing interest in movies produced locally. These films often reflect things they can relate to, unlike those imported from Hollywood. The quality of South Korean films has also increased foreign interest, and producers are seeing higher international sales as a result.

**People walk by a poster for the 2006 South Korean film *The Host*, one of the top-grossing South Korean movies of all time.**

# CHAPTER 7
# POLITICS: CHALLENGING CORRUPTION

The first constitution of South Korea was adopted on July 17, 1948. Influenced by the United States, it stated that the Republic of Korea would be a democratic republic. The document guaranteed freedom of speech, the press, and assembly. It placed importance on equal access to education for all citizens, and it forbade unlawful searches. However, parts of the document resulted in many of the political problems the country faced moving forward. One article permitted the government to restrict the rights of citizens if deemed necessary to maintain public order, meaning that those in power could legally prohibit people from enjoying the freedoms listed in the constitution. Unfortunately, this happened often between the end of the Korean War and the late 1980s.

**The South Korean flag**

**The Korean National Assembly building in Seoul**

The constitution was also frequently amended to favor the existing power structure, particularly as it pertained to presidential terms and powers. The last and eighth time the constitution was rewritten was in 1987, but this time the revisions favored the people. Key amendments involved the restriction of presidential powers and the limiting of presidents to a single five-year term. The National Assembly was given impeachment powers over the president, the prime minister, and judges. And the provisions from the first constitution that allowed for the removal of rights and freedoms were eliminated.

## STRUCTURE OF THE GOVERNMENT OF SOUTH KOREA

| Executive Branch | Legislative Branch | Judicial Branch |
|---|---|---|
| President<br>Prime Minister | National Assembly | Supreme Court<br>Constitutional Court<br>appellate courts<br>local courts |

## BRANCHES OF GOVERNMENT

The Republic of Korea's government is broken into three branches: the executive, the legislative, and the judicial. The executive branch includes the president, the chief of state who is elected by the South Korean people for a single five-year term. This branch also includes the prime minister, who is the head of government. The prime minister is appointed by the president and approved by the National Assembly.

The National Assembly, the core of the legislative branch of government, consists of 299 members elected to four-year terms. Most are elected by popular vote, but 54 are distributed among political parties based on the results of the election. The legislative assembly is convened once a year for a maximum of 100 days. For the first several decades of South Korea's history, the country was effectively a police state run by dictators, and the National Assembly did the bidding of the president. In recent decades, following the constitutional reforms, South Koreans have seen a better representation of their views in the National Assembly.

The judicial branch is the third branch of government. It is made up of the Supreme Court, the Constitutional Court, appellate courts, and local courts. In both the Supreme Court and the Constitutional Court, justices are appointed by the president, with consent and guidance from the National Assembly. Justices in both courts serve six-year renewable terms, except for the chief justice of the Supreme Court, who cannot be reappointed.

The elections of 2012 marked the first time in 20 years that elections for the National

## POLITICAL PARTIES

The dynamic and rapidly changing political landscape of South Korea has led to an ever-changing sea of political parties. Former rivals join together to create new alliances, and old parties change names to give themselves a fresh look. The New Frontier Party, a conservative party and the biggest winners in the 2012 National Assembly election, was once called the Grand National Party. The biggest opposition party, the liberal Democratic United Party, was previously known as the Democratic Party. Two smaller parties ran and won seats in the 2012 elections, the liberal Unified Progressive Party and the conservative Advancement Unification Party.

Assembly and the presidential elections took place in the same year. In April 2012, the New Frontier Party, led by Park Geun Hye, the daughter of former president Park Chung Hee, won the majority of seats in the National Assembly. In July 2012, Park announced she would be running for president in December 2012. The prime minister of South Korea in 2012 was Kim Hwang Sik. He was confirmed by the National Assembly in October 2010.

## CORRUPTION

One of the biggest challenges South Korea has faced within the government is corruption. Some analysts have referred to South Korea's problem as a culture of corruption, where old-fashioned loyalties, personal guarantees, and familial relationships are more important than contractual or legal agreements. Slipping an envelope of cash into the hand of a government official in order to gain favor of some kind is not uncommon.

The problem has proven difficult to solve. Several successive presidents have made promises to crack down on corruption, only to be accused of questionable activities themselves. President Chun Doo Hwan and his successor Roh Tae Woo both went to trial in 1996, during the presidency of Kim Young Sam, faced with allegations of personally pocketing hundreds of millions of dollars in election donations. Chun and Roh both went to jail, but later that year, President Kim and his son were accused of accepting bribes. The tradition continued with Kim

Young Sam's successor, Kim Dae Jung. His three sons were also found guilty of accepting payoffs in 2003.

South Korea's next president, Roh Moo Hyun, pledged to crack down on corruption. During his time as president Roh was known as "Mr. Clean." Within a year after the end of his presidency, several members of Roh's family, including his wife, children, and brother, were accused of accepting bribes that were alleged to have passed through to Roh himself. The investigation led to Roh taking his own life in May 2009. That same year, the ROK ranked twenty-second out of 30 major countries listed on the Global Corruption Index of the Organisation for Economic Co-operation and Development.[1] President Lee Myung Bak's term has also been tainted by accusations of corruption; three of his cabinet appointees were forced to resign because of allegations of accepting bribes.

## FOREIGN RELATIONS

Though it was once known as a hermit kingdom, South Korea now has diplomatic relations with 170 nations around the globe. It has been

**Corruption is a pervasive problem in the South Korean government.**

a member of the UN since August 1991, and it has hosted several international events and summits since the 1980s. The United States maintains strong military and economic ties to South Korea. Under the 1953 Mutual Defense Treaty, the United States agreed to help the Republic of Korea defend itself against external aggression; for this purpose, the United States maintains military personnel in South Korea, including an army division and several air force tactical squadrons. A total of approximately 28,000 personnel are stationed there.[3] South Korea also has ties with Japan, and the two countries cooperate frequently on a number of issues that are of importance to both nations, including security of the peninsula and common waterways. However, intense popular antagonism between the two nations still exists, a lasting effect of the Japanese occupation of the Korean Peninsula.

The relationship between South Korea and North Korea remains damaged. Many attempts have been made over the years to bring the two Koreas closer together, including the Pyongyang summit in 2000, but provocations still occur frequently. North Korea's tests of nuclear weapons in 2006 and 2009 brought strong condemnations from not only South Korea, but also many other nations. In 2010, North Korea torpedoed a South Korean ship in the Yellow Sea, killing 46.[4] North Korea denied responsibility, but international observers agreed they sank the ship. Later that year, following South Korean artillery training exercises, North Korea fired artillery and rockets at a South Korean island near the

**An American soldier and two South Korean soldiers stand at an observation post near the DMZ.**

border between the two nations. The attack killed two South Koreans and injured more than a dozen more.[5] The North Korean military claimed the attack was in response to the South Korean exercises. In the spring of 2012, South Korea issued a stern warning to North Korea in response to a planned missile test by the North. Despite this warning, North Korea went ahead with the launch, claiming they were only putting a satellite in space for scientific research. Though the rocket failed, the Korean Peninsula remained in a very unstable state.

South Korea is also making sure that it is being heard on important global issues. In 2010, it hosted the leaders of several major countries, as well as heads of the International Monetary Fund and the World Bank at the G20 Summit in Seoul. In October 2011, President Lee Myung Bak hosted the Korea-Japan Summit in the capital city. At this summit, as a gesture of reconciliation, Japan returned hundreds of volumes of royal books from the Choson dynasty that had been taken when Japan occupied the peninsula. Two years after the G20 Summit, the ROK hosted 50 national leaders at the 2012 Seoul Nuclear Security Summit. The objective of the summit was to create coordinated efforts to tackle the problem of keeping nuclear material out of the hands of terrorists and rogue states.

**Pyeongchang will host the 2018 Winter Olympics.**

**The president of South Korea in 2012 was Lee Myung Bak.**

amounts of financial aid. Supporting the United States in the Vietnam War also brought revenue to the ROK; the money helped Park finance South Korea's development.

Park's policies are generally considered economically effective, but the Korean people must also be given credit. Much of the workforce shifted from agriculture to industry. Many worked long hours at low wages in new industries to support growth and development. South Koreans also took advantage of the government's education reforms. At the end of World War II, only approximately 20 percent of the population was educated; 60 years later, approximately 98 percent of the population was able to read and write.[4] This allowed many more people to find skilled work.

## THE SOUTH KOREAN WON

The South Korean currency is the South Korean won. The name means "round shape," and is related to words for the Japanese and Chinese currencies, called yen and yuan respectively. The current South Korean won was introduced in 1962. Coins feature images of Korean symbols, including turtle ships and stalks of rice. Beginning in 2006, new banknotes were introduced, with new security features to prevent counterfeiting. The banknotes feature portraits of notable Koreans from throughout history. In 2012, 1,000 won was worth approximately US$0.86.

**Korean currency is produced by the Korean Minting and Security Printing Corporation.**

## CHAEBOL

All of the major corporations in South Korea are *chaebol*, or very large, family-run conglomerates. When Park Chung Hee was president, his economic policies favored the chaebol and allowed them to borrow more money from the state-run banks than smaller competitors. This gave these companies the opportunity to grow. At the same time, it made it difficult for smaller companies not supported by the government to compete. Over time, as the chaebol grew larger, they gained more influence over government. The major chaebol have often been involved with South Korea's corruption cases. Automakers Hyundai Motor Group and Kia and electronics companies Samsung and LG are among the largest chaebol.

# LABOR FORCE AND EMPLOYMENT

The country's 25 million-strong workforce is the twenty-fifth largest in the world.[5] The service industry employs 70 percent of these people, accounting for 60 percent of the GDP.[6] The overall unemployment rate was relatively low in 2011, with only 3.4 percent of willing workers unable to find a job.[7]

Still, South Korea's rising economy has not benefitted all citizens. It is estimated that one-quarter of the population lives in what Korea defines as absolute poverty, meaning they earn less than the minimum required to cover the cost of living.[8] Elderly divorced or widowed women are particularly affected by this problem. It is estimated that as many as 45 percent of senior citizens live in poverty.[9] Employment equity is also a problem. Women are hired less often than men, increasing women's chances of falling into poverty.

Additionally, many employees are working without an employment contract, which means they have little job security. They can be fired with no notice and no severance pay. Also, as is the case in many developed nations, the income disparity between rich and poor is growing.

## INDUSTRY AND RESOURCES

Some of the biggest names in automobiles, consumer electronics, and information technology have come from South Korea. In many cases, South Korean companies have come from behind to take over market share from their much more established global competitors. South Korea is the world's fifth-largest automobile producer, the top producer of semiconductors and computer displays, and the second-biggest producer of cell phones.[10] They are also a major shipbuilding country.

Before the Korean War, the vast majority of the population worked the land to earn their living and feed the population. By 2011, however, approximately 6 percent of the population worked in agriculture, and their work accounted for only 2.6 percent of the GDP.[11] The primary crop is rice. Livestock production, including cattle, pigs and chickens, is now the second-largest agricultural sector behind rice. Fishing was once a major source of income and food for many people, but overfishing led to depleted stocks, and in 1997 South Korea passed a Fishery Act that put limits on catches. Other crops include barley, wheat, and soybeans, but

> **South Korea accounts for 34 percent of the ships built globally.**

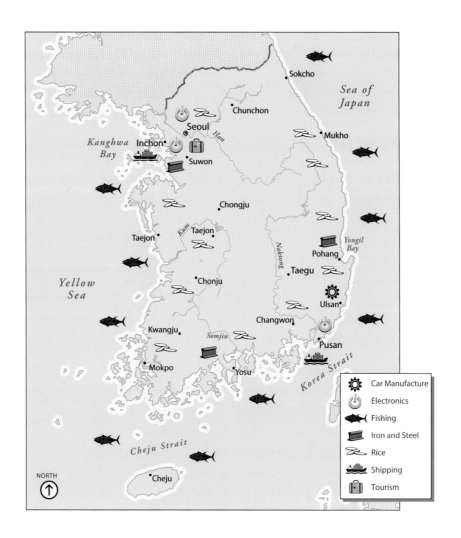

**Resources of South Korea**

diversity of crops has declined along with the decline of the industry. Still, farmers produce enough fruits and vegetables to supply the population.

## IMPORTS AND EXPORTS

South Korea sends semiconductors, telecommunications equipment, vehicles, computers, steel, ships, and petrochemicals to their largest trading partners, which include China, the United States, Japan, and the European Union (EU). In 2011, South Korea exported more than US$556 billion worth of goods, ranking it the eighth-largest exporter in the world.[12]

One of the weaknesses of the South Korean economy is this reliance on exports. Almost one-quarter of South Korea's products go to China, and another 10 percent go to the United States.[13] Economic downturns in either of these countries can have a dramatic impact on South Korea's economy.

### FREE TRADE AGREEMENT

In March 2012, after several years of negotiation, the United States and South Korea Free Trade Agreement went into effect. Before the agreement, the South Korean government placed much higher tariffs on US goods coming into its country than the United States placed on South Korean goods coming into the United States. This put US manufacturers at a disadvantage. Under the new agreement, most US goods entering into South Korea are now duty-free. Both the South Korean and US governments describe the agreement as a job creator for each of their nations.

In recent years, South Korea has worked hard to improve relations with its trading partners in hopes of increasing overall trade. In 2011, it entered into a free trade agreement with the EU. March 2012 marked the beginning of a new free trade agreement with the United States, and in May 2012, Japan, China, and South Korea agreed to begin negotiations on a trilateral free trade agreement.

South Korea is also heavily dependent on imports. Machinery, electronics, transportation equipment, plastics, and organic chemicals are imported from China, Japan, the United States, and Australia. South Korea is a huge importer of oil, too. It also must import large quantities of coal and natural gas.

## INFRASTRUCTURE AND TRANSPORTATION

Paved roadways, express highways, railways, subways, ports, and airports all saw dramatic expansion between 1960 and 2010. People and goods now move throughout the country more easily and freely than ever before. In 1988, there were only approximately 15,500 miles (25,000 km) of paved roadways and just more than 930 miles (1,500 km) of expressways. By 2008, there were more than 49,000 miles (80,000 km) of paved roads and 2,000 miles (3,367 km) of expressways.[14] Although the roads have made travel easier in some ways, the corresponding increase

**South Korea has a strong shipping industry.**

in the number of vehicles on the road has led to complaints of gridlock, especially in large cities such as Seoul and Pusan.

With the growth in trade activity, South Korea's seaports have also expanded. Pusan is home to one of the world's largest container ports. Situated on the southwest tip of the peninsula, it is only 110 nautical miles from Japan and serves as South Korea's gateway to the Pacific. Pusan handles 40 percent of South Korea's overseas cargo and 80 percent of its container cargo, as well as 40 percent of its fisheries production. The port welcomes 130 marine vessels each day.[15] And container trade is growing, showing an 8 percent increase from June 2010 to June 2011.[16]

> In 2011, South Korea exceeded US$1 trillion in foreign trade, the ninth country ever to do so.

## TOURISM

Drawn to the beautiful beaches, numerous World Heritage Sites, and hundreds of Buddhist temples, visitors from all over the world come to enjoy what South Korea has to offer. More than 34 percent of foreign visitors come from Japan and another 20 percent come from China.[17] Their visits, along with those of people from Europe, the United States, and Taiwan, help keep 1.38 million South Koreans employed in hotels, travel agencies, airlines, and other tourism-related service

**South Korea's advanced transportation systems, including subways, have greatly improved both personal mobility and international trade.**

industries.[18] Tourism added more than KRW 22,946 billion into the economy in 2011, contributing 1.8 percent to the total GDP.[19] The revenue generated from tourist visits is expected to grow an average of 3.5 percent per year until 2022.[20]

## UNESCO WORLD HERITAGE SITES

South Korea's long history has left it with a large number of historically significant sites, which can be major selling points for interested tourists. UNESCO has registered ten sites in South Korea as World Heritage Sites. Among the heritage sites is the Changdeokgung Palace. Built in the early 1400s by King Sejong, it is an excellent example of a Far Eastern palace. It is also recognized for how harmoniously it fits into its irregularly shaped 143-acre (58 ha) property.[21]

**South Korea heavily promotes tourism within the country. Destinations include historic sites such as this temple in the country's southwest.**

## CHAPTER 9
# SOUTH KOREA TODAY

South Korea has proven itself to be a very adaptable, hardworking nation. If the devastation of war, the abuses of leaders and government officials, the turmoil of the global economy, and the threats of its sister nation have not been able to slow the country down, then it is difficult to imagine what will. Since South Korea finally became a truly democratic country, government leaders have worked diligently to open the country to the world and improve its image. They continue to make strides toward this goal.

## SOUTH KOREAN TEENS

The everyday lives of normal South Koreans have played a critical role in the nation's march into modernity, and citizens see their lives as being linked to the country's welfare. South Koreans are dedicated to education, and believe it to be the key to both individual and national

**Two boys wear brightly colored traditional clothing.**

> **A student expression says if one sleeps more than four hours a night, one will not gain entry to a university.**

success. There is no better example of this than on the day of the College Scholastic Ability Test (CSAT). Students take this test in their final year of high school. Each November, hundreds of thousands of high school students across South Korea sit down on the same day at exactly the same time to complete the test. The entire country is put on hold to ensure students arrive at school on time and have the peace and quiet they need to concentrate on the exam. On this day there are extra buses and subways running to transport students. Police officers even drive students to school. Motorists are not permitted to honk their horns, planes are rerouted or delayed, and the stock market opens an hour late. Younger students start gathering at the schools long before the test takers arrive; they hold up posters with encouraging messages for the senior students and cheer loudly when they arrive. And parents pray for their child's success. How students perform on the CSAT will determine which university they attend, which in turn will determine their career path. The university a student chooses to attend will also likely determine his or her spouse, because many South Koreans socialize with and marry people from the same university they attended. Children spend their entire school life preparing to take the CSAT.

Education in South Korea is equally available to all. Children start elementary school at the age of six, but many attend two or three years of kindergarten before this. Almost all schools are public, and courses

**South Korean students take their studies very seriously.**

and textbooks are paid for by the government. More than 80 percent of high school students move on to postsecondary education.[1] The average student has a total of 17 years of education.[2]

This focus on education does not leave the average South Korean teen with a lot of leisure time, but when teens do have spare time, they spend it engaging in many of the same pastimes American teens do. They are a high-tech country, so text messaging, social media, video games, music, and movies are an important part of their daily lives.

More than in any other part of society, the influences of modernization can be seen in the South Korean popular culture scene. It is with astounding speed that South Korea has moved from the ruin of the Korean War to becoming the trendsetter of Asia. Japanese and Chinese teens in particular clamor to get at anything South Korean. Korean movies, television shows, and music are all finding an international audience they never had in the past. And the K-pop genre of music has swept the world.

## PUBLIC DISPLAYS OF AFFECTION

It is common to see two boys or two girls walking hand in hand or with their arms around each other's shoulders in public; this is a sign of friendship. However, it is considered inappropriate for a man and woman to show too much romantic affection in public, and others will often show their disapproval.

**A motorcycle policeman gives a late student a ride to the CSAT.**

Recognizing the economic benefits of a strong media and entertainment sector, the government is now supporting and sponsoring this industry just as it has many others over the years. It even promotes singing groups on official government Web sites.

## CURRENT CHALLENGES

Despite a relatively bright outlook, South Korea does still face some challenges in a number of areas. Corruption remains a problem despite the strong punishments against previous offenders. The citizens are becoming more vocal about this, as well as about the extensive powers of large corporations, poor working conditions, and low wages. They have shown they are prepared

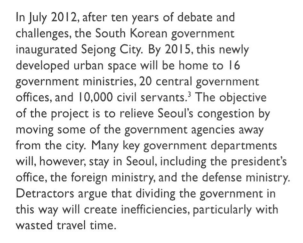

### NEW "MINI-CAPITAL"

In July 2012, after ten years of debate and challenges, the South Korean government inaugurated Sejong City. By 2015, this newly developed urban space will be home to 16 government ministries, 20 central government offices, and 10,000 civil servants.[3] The objective of the project is to relieve Seoul's congestion by moving some of the government agencies away from the city. Many key government departments will, however, stay in Seoul, including the president's office, the foreign ministry, and the defense ministry. Detractors argue that dividing the government in this way will create inefficiencies, particularly with wasted travel time.

**South Koreans protest poor working conditions in 2006.**

**South Korean seniors look for jobs at an employment fair in 2003.**

to rise up against authority to force change. If the government is not proactive about improving some of these things, it could face more public demonstrations, especially as elections approach.

South Korea's commitment to the environment is also sometimes questioned. Many developments, such as the river restoration projects, have environmentalists worried the South Korean government is more concerned with the short-term needs of its people than with the long-term protection of animals and nature. Pollution and overpopulation in cities are still problems, too. The government must strike a balance between continued economic growth, meeting the needs of the people, and taking care of the environment.

Taking care of the aging population is also a big concern for the future. A vast number of people will be entering into retirement over the next 35 years. The younger generation is not having as many children, so there are concerns there will not be enough people to replace retirees. Fewer births also means there will be fewer people to care for the elderly. Many of the country's old people already live in poverty, and unless the government works to establish a solid social safety net for these people

## SIGNIFICANT BIRTHDAY CELEBRATIONS

In South Korea, the first 100 days of a child's life are considered to be fragile. Usually, only immediate family members see the mother and baby in the first months after delivery, and it is rare to give a gift at the birth of the baby. On the one-hundredth day, however, it is considered safe for the baby to receive visitors and venture out into the world. This is when neighbors, friends, and coworkers will usually visit and bring gifts. In adulthood, the grandest birthday celebration is *hwangab*, held at age 60. In the lunar calendar there are only 60 names for years, so South Koreans believe that at 60 the calendar returns to your birth year and begins a new cycle.

and address the low population growth, this problem may continue to get worse.

South Korea is, however, becoming a more vocal participant in international affairs and a growing influence in global culture. The younger generation is well prepared to take their country into the future and expand on the achievements and success of their parents and grandparents. South Korea has made it clear to the rest of the world they are a country to pay attention to in the twenty-first century.

**South Koreans look forward to a bright future.**

# TIMELINE

| 8000 BCE | Early Korean cultures settle on the Korean Peninsula. |
|---|---|
| ca. 400 BCE | The Choson Kingdom thrives on the peninsula. |
| ca. 100 BCE | The kingdoms of Koguryo, Paekche, and Silla are established. |
| 668 CE | With the help of the Chinese, Silla takes over the entire Korean Peninsula. |
| 918 | Wang Kon founds the Koryo dynasty. |
| 1392 | Yi Song Gye establishes the Choson dynasty. Under the Yi family reign, Choson was the longest-lasting Korean dynasty. |
| 1592 | Japan invades the Korean Peninsula, but Korean forces armed with "turtle ships" defeat them. |
| 1876 | Korea signs an unequal treaty with Japan that gives Japanese nationals territorial rights and opens three Korean ports to trade with Japan. |
| 1904 | The Russo-Japanese War begins, leading to Japanese rule over the Korean Peninsula. |
| 1910 | Japan annexes the Korean Peninsula and controls it until the end of World War II. |
| 1945 | After World War II, the US and the Soviet Union divide the Korean Peninsula at the 38th parallel. |
| 1948 | On May 10, Syngman Rhee is elected the first president of South Korea. |

| | |
|---|---|
| 1950 | On June 25, Kim Il Sung crosses the 38th parallel and invades the Republic of Korea. |
| 1953 | On July 27, an armistice is signed and a demilitarized zone along the 38th parallel is established. |
| 1960 | The Student Revolution results in the deaths of 142 people. |
| 1961 | A military coup overthrows the ruling Democratic Party, beginning 32 years of military rule in South Korea. |
| 1979 | On October 26, President Park Chung Hee is assassinated. |
| 1988 | South Korea hosts the Summer Olympic Games in Seoul. |
| 1993 | In February, Kim Young Sam is elected president in the first truly free democratic election in South Korea's history. |
| 1997 | South Korea experiences a severe economic crisis. |
| 1998 | Kim Dae Jung is the first opposition party leader elected president. |
| 2000 | President Kim Dae Jung meets with North Korean leader Kim Jong Il. |
| 2003 | Roh Moo Hyun becomes president. |
| 2008 | Lee Myung Bak, a former Hyundai executive and mayor of Seoul, becomes president of South Korea. |

# FACTS AT YOUR FINGERTIPS

## GEOGRAPHY

Official name: Republic of Korea

Area: 38,502 square miles
(99,720 sq km)

Climate: Cold, dry winters and hot,
humid summers.

Highest elevation: Mount Halla,
6,398 feet (1,950 m) above sea level

Lowest elevation: Sea of Japan,
0 feet (0 m) below sea level

Significant geographic features:
dominated by hills and mountains
with wide coastal plains to the west
and south

## PEOPLE

Population: 48,860,500
(July 2012 est.)

Most populous city: Seoul

Ethnic groups: Korean except for
approximately 20,000 Chinese

Percentage of residents living in
urban areas: 83 percent

Life expectancy: 79.3
(world rank: 41)

Languages: Korean and English

Religions: Buddhist, 32 percent;
Christian, 26.3 percent (Protestant,
19.7 percent; Roman Catholic,
6.6 percent); other or unknown,
1.3 percent; none, 49.3 percent
(1995 census)

## GOVERNMENT AND ECONOMY

Government: republic

Capital: Seoul

Date of adoption of current constitution: July 17, 1948, most recently amended October 29, 1987

Head of state: president

Head of government: prime minister

Legislature: National Assembly

Currency: South Korean won

Industries and natural resources: electronics, automobile production, shipbuilding, steel, coal, lead, rice, vegetables, cattle, fish

## NATIONAL SYMBOLS

Holidays: Memorial Day, celebrated on June 6, commemorates those who died in military service. Constitution Day, on July 17, celebrates the founding of the Republic of Korea.

Flag: The Taegukki features a white background with a red and blue yin-yang symbol in the center. The symbol is surrounded by four black trigrams, each representing one of four universal elements.

National anthem: "Aegukga" ("Patriotic Song")

National flower: mugunghwa (rose of Sharon)

## KEY PEOPLE

Syngman Rhee (1875–1965) was the first president of South Korea; he amended the constitution several times in order to remain in power for 12 years from 1948 to 1960.

Park Chung Hee (1917–1979), a military general, was South Korea's longest-serving president.

Lee Myung Bak (1941–), formerly a car company executive and mayor of Seoul, became South Korea's president in 2008. His term was scheduled to end in 2013.

## PLACES TO VISIT

*If you are ever in South Korea, consider checking out these important and interesting sites!*

### Baekundong Valley

This scenic valley is home to many waterfalls and hidden ponds. The highest waterfall, Baekun, is approximately 100 feet (30 m) high. It is a popular spot for mountain climbers.

### The Demilitarized Zone (DMZ)

A trip to the peninsula must include a visit to the DMZ. From the iron and barbed wire fences to the breathtaking untouched land, the world's most heavily guarded border is a fascinating place.

### Hwaseong Fortress

Located in Gyeonggi Province, Hwaseong Fortress is a walled city from the Choson dynasty. It was registered as a UNESCO World Heritage Site in 1997.

### The Korean Folk Village

Also located in Gyeonggi Province, the Korean Folk Village offers visitors a glimpse into Korea's past. More than 260 traditional houses can be viewed, along with a number of workshops and handcrafts such as pottery, musical instruments, fans, paper, and ironware.

# SOURCE NOTES

### CHAPTER 1. A VISIT TO SOUTH KOREA

1. "Seoul." *Encyclopædia Britannica*. Encyclopædia Britannica, 2012. Web. 14 Sept. 2012.

2. "Myeong-dong." *Korea*. Korean Tourism Organization, n.d. Web. 14 Sept. 2012.

3. Ibid.

### CHAPTER 2. GEOGRAPHY: A VIRTUAL ISLAND

1. "The World Factbook: South Korea." *Central Intelligence Agency*. Central Intelligence Agency, 10 Sept. 2012. Web. 14 Sept. 2012.

2. Ibid.

3. "Sea of Japan." *Encyclopædia Britannica*. Encyclopædia Britannica, 2012. Web. 14 Sept. 2012.

4. Mary E. Connor. *The Koreas*. Santa Barbara, CA: ABC-CLIO, 2009. Print. 6.

5. Violet Kim, Gigi Ban, and Sunny Kim. "33 Beautiful Islands to Visit in Korea." *CNN Go*. CNN, 3 Aug. 2012. Web. 17 Sept. 2012.

6. "Cheju Island." *Encyclopædia Britannica*. Encyclopædia Britannica, 2012. Web. 17 Sept. 2012.

7. "South Korea." *Weatherbase*. Canty and Associates, 2012. Web. 17 Sept. 2012.

8. "Snowstorm Sweeps Across S. Korea." *CCTV English*. CCTV, 15 Feb. 2011. Web. 17 Sept. 2012.

9. "The World Factbook: South Korea." *Central Intelligence Agency*. Central Intelligence Agency, 10 Sept. 2012. Web. 17 Sept. 2012.

10. Ibid.

11. "South Korea." *World Port Source*. World Port Source, 2012. Web. 17 Sept. 2012.

12. Ibid.

### CHAPTER 3. ANIMALS AND NATURE: ENDANGERED BY DEVELOPMENT

1. "Fauna and Flora." *Ministry of Environment*. Republic of Korea Ministry of Environment, n.d. Web. 17 Sept. 2012.

2. "MOE to Expand Endangered Wild Fauna And Flora to 246 Species." *Ministry of Environment*. Republic of Korea Ministry of Environment, 31 May 2012. Web. 17 Sept. 2012.

3. "Fauna and Flora." *Ministry of Environment*. Republic of Korea Ministry of Environment, n.d. Web. 17 Sept. 2012.

4. "Summary Statistics: Summaries by Country, Table 5, Threatened Species in Each Country." *IUCN Red List of Threatened Species*. International Union for Conservation of Nature and Natural Resources, 2011. Web. 17 Sept. 2012.

5. "Fauna and Flora." *Ministry of Environment*. Republic of Korea Ministry of Environment, n.d. Web. 17 Sept. 2012.

6. "South Korea Market Profile." *South Carolina Forestry Commission*. South Carolina Forestry Commission, n.d. Web. 17 Sept. 2012.

7. Jon Herskovitz. "South Korea Green Growth to Hurt Environment: Report." *Reuters*. Reuters, 18 Mar. 2010. Web. 17 Sept. 2012.

8. "The Air Quality Index for Seoul, South Korea." *Environmental Performance Index*. Asian Institute for Environmental and Energy Studies, 25 Jan. 2012. Web. 17 Sept. 2012.

9. Ibid.

10. "Natural Park." *Ministry of Environment*. Republic of Korea Ministry of Environment, n.d. Web. 17 Sept. 2012.

11. Tony Azios. "Korean Demilitarized Zone Now A Wildlife Haven." *Christian Science Monitor*. Christian Science Monitor, 21 Nov. 2008. Web. 17 Sept. 2012.

12. Mary E. Connor. *The Koreas*. Santa Barbara, CA: ABC-CLIO, 2009. Print. 4.

13. "Ecology and Scenery Conservation Area." *Ministry of Environment*. Republic of Korea Ministry of Environment, n.d. Web. 17 Sept. 2012.

## CHAPTER 4. HISTORY: A NATION DIVIDED

1. "Haeinsa Temple." *Korea*. Korean Tourism Organization, n.d. Web. 17 Sept. 2012.

2. "A Country Study: South Korea." *Library of Congress*. Library of Congress, 22 Mar. 2011. Web. 17 Sept. 2012.

3. Ibid.

4. Ibid.

5. Ibid.

6. "South Korea." *Encyclopædia Britannica*. Encyclopædia Britannica, 2012. Web. 17 Sept. 2012.

7. Mary E. Connor. *The Koreas*. Santa Barbara, CA: ABC-CLIO, 2009. Print. 83.

8. "Voter Turnout Data for Republic of Korea." *Voter Turnout*. International Institute for Democracy and Electoral Assistance, 5 Oct. 2011. Web. 17 Sept. 2012.

## CHAPTER 5. PEOPLE: AN AGING POPULATION

1. "Country Comparison: Birth Rate." *Central Intelligence Agency*. Central Intelligence Agency, 10 Sept. 2012. Web. 17 Sept. 2012.

2. "The World Factbook: South Korea." *Central Intelligence Agency*. Central Intelligence Agency, 10 Sept. 2012. Web. 17 Sept. 2012.

3. Ibid.

4. Ibid.

5. Mary E. Connor. *The Koreas*. Santa Barbara, CA: ABC-CLIO, 2009. Print. 186.

# SOURCE NOTES CONTINUED

6. "The World Factbook." *Central Intelligence Agency*. Central Intelligence Agency, 10 Sept. 2012. Web. 17 Sept. 2012.

7. "Seoul." *Encyclopædia Britannica*. Encyclopædia Britannica, 2012. Web. 14 Sept. 2012.

8. "The World Factbook: South Korea." *Central Intelligence Agency*. Central Intelligence Agency, 10 Sept. 2012. Web. 17 Sept. 2012.

9. Ibid.

10. James Hoare. *Culture Smart! Korea*. Portland, OR: Graphic Arts Center Publishing Company, 2005. Print. 150–152.

11. Mary E. Connor. *The Koreas*. Santa Barbara, CA: ABC-CLIO, 2009. Print. 227.

12. "The World Factbook: South Korea." *Central Intelligence Agency*. Central Intelligence Agency, 10 Sept. 2012. Web. 17 Sept. 2012

### CHAPTER 6. CULTURE: HOLDING ON TO TRADITIONS
1. "2002 FIFA World Cup Korea/Japan." *Korea.net*. Korea.net, 2012. Web. 17 Sept. 2012.

2. "Park Tae-hwan Is Too Young to Give Up." *Chosunilbo*. Chosun Media, 29 July 2009. Web. 17 Sept. 2012.

3. "Republic of Korea." *Medals*. Official London 2012 Website, 2012. Web. 17 Sept. 2012.

### CHAPTER 7. POLITICS: CHALLENGING CORRUPTION
1. Park Si-soo. "Korea Ranks 39th in Global Corruption Index." *Korea Times*. Korea Times, 17 Nov. 2009. Web. 17 Sept. 2012.

2. Donald Kirk. "Confucianist Corruption in South Korea." *Asia Times Online*. Asia Times, 14 May 2009. Web. 17 Sept. 2012.

3. "Background Note: South Korea." *US Department of State*. US Department of State, 12 Apr. 2012. Web. 17 Sept. 2012.

4. Choe Sang-Hun. "South Korea Publicly Blames the North for Ship's Sinking." *New York Times*. New York Times, 19 May 2012. Web. 17 Sept. 2012.

5. Mark McDonald. "'Crisis Status' in South Korea After North Shells Island." *New York Times*. New York Times, 23 Nov. 2010. Web. 17 Sept. 2012.

### CHAPTER 8. ECONOMICS: ASTONISHING GROWTH
1. Mark Weisbrot and Rebecca Ray. "The Scorecard on Development, 1960–2010: Closing the Gap?" *DESA Working Paper No. 106*. UN Department of Economic and Social Affairs, June 2011. Web. 18 Sept. 2012.

2. "The World Factbook: South Korea." *Central Intelligence Agency*. Central Intelligence Agency, 10 Sept. 2012. Web. 18 Sept. 2012

3. Uk Heo and Terence Roehrig. *South Korea Since 1980*. New York: Cambridge UP, 2011. Print. 21.

4. "A Country Study: South Korea." *Library of Congress*. Library of Congress, 22 Mar. 2011. Web. 18 Sept. 2012.

5. "The World Factbook: South Korea." *Central Intelligence Agency*. Central Intelligence Agency, 10 Sept. 2012. Web. 18 Sept. 2012.

6. Ibid.

7. Ibid.

8. "One Quarter of South Koreans Touched by Poverty." *Radio Australia*. ABC, 13 Feb. 2012. Web. 18 Sept. 2012.

9. Jack Kim and Ju-min Park. "Analysis: South Korea's Unloved Chaebol." *Reuters*. Reuters, 5 Apr. 2012. Web. 18 Sept. 2012.

10. "Economic Situation." *Korea.net*. Korea.net, 2012. Web. 18 Sept. 2012.

11. "The World Factbook: South Korea." *Central Intelligence Agency*. Central Intelligence Agency, 10 Sept. 2012. Web. 18 Sept. 2012.

12. Ibid.

13. Ibid.

14. "A Country Study: South Korea." *Library of Congress*. Library of Congress, 22 Mar. 2011. Web. 18 Sept. 2012.

15. "About Pusan." *AboutCrew*. AboutCrew, 2011. Web. 18 Sept. 2012.

16. "Container Trade Volume in Korean Ports." *Korea.net*. Korea.net, 2012. Web. 18 Sept. 2012.

17. "Travel Information." *Korea.net*. Korea.net, 2012. Web. 18 Sept. 2012.

18. "Travel and Tourism Economic Impact 2012: South Korea." *World Travel & Tourism Council*. World Travel & Tourism Council, 2012. Web. 18 Sept. 2012.

19. Ibid.

20. Ibid.

21. "Changdeokgung Palace Complex." *World Heritage List*. UNESCO, 2012. Web. 18 Sept. 2012.

## CHAPTER 9. SOUTH KOREA TODAY

1. Jiyeon Lee. "South Korean Students' 'Year of Hell' Culminates with Exams Day." *CNN*. CNN, 10 Nov. 2011. Web. 18 Sept. 2012.

2. "The World Factbook: South Korea." *Central Intelligence Agency*. Central Intelligence Agency, 10 Sept. 2012. Web. 18 Sept. 2012.

3. "S. Korea to Open Controversial New Mini Capital." *Sun Daily*. Sun Daily, 1 July 2012. Web. 18 Sept. 2012.

# INDEX

## PHOTO CREDITS

Andrey Shchekalev/Shutterstock Images, cover, 63; Gina Smith/Shutterstock Images, 2, 70, 116; iStockphoto, 5 (top), 13, 69, 79, 81, 110, 113; Keith Brooks/Shutterstock Images, 5 (center), 35; iStockphoto/Thinkstock, 5 (bottom), 14, 28, 31, 37, 88, 90, 104, 131, 132; Shutterstock Images, 6, 9, 20, 42, 83; Matt Kania/Map Hero, Inc., 10, 19, 24, 61, 108; Dae Seung Seo/Getty Images, 16; Thinkstock, 27, 130; Maxim Tupikov/Shutterstock Images, 32, 74; Jang Seung Hoon/AFP/Getty Images, 38, 128 (top); Bettmann/Corbis/AP Images, 45, 103; AP Images, 46, 51, 128 (bottom), 129 (top); John Dominis/Getty Images, 53; Cornelius Poppe/AP Images, 57, 129 (bottom); EdStock/iStockphoto, 58, 98, 119; Ahn Young-joon/AP Images, 67, 85, 94; Lee Jin-man/AP Images, 73, 86, 121, 123; Hye Soo Nah/AP Images, 77; Edward N. Johnson, U.S. Army Public Affairs Officer, 97; Ingram Publishing/Thinkstock, 100, 133; Ed Wray/AP Images, 114; Yun Jai-hyoung/AP Images, 124; Kyodo/AP Images, 127